girovagando in Puglia

1

GELSOROSSO

roaming about

ALBEROBELLO

Alberobello, the city of the "trulli"

Introduction

The origins of the city date back to the second half of XVIth, when the little feud under the Acquaviva family, Counts of Conversano, was populated of farmers cultivating the (so called) "Selva".
Farmers were allowed to build houses but they were prohibited to use any type of mortar; this way the counts could demolish the houses and expel the colonists whenever they wanted.
The prohibition was also a dictate of "Prammatica of baronibus", wanted by Aragona's family and handed on during Spanish rule; It prohibited barons to build any new urban conglomeration, without the Royal blessing: "acciò villa e non terra, né castello fosse quel luogo riputato, né inducesse giammai al barone la pena della prammatica".
Here it is the main reason for the prohibition of the manufacting in lime: the improvised houses, called "casedde", were temporary, and in case of royal inspection they needed to be demolished as fast as possible, disseminating stones in the coutryside.
Despite this serious awe, due to the whim of

the count but above all to tax laws of the kingdom, the population grew up thanks to the immunities and the exemption that the count granted them.

In 1797 a group of brave citizens of Alberobello, getting tired of precarious conditions, went to Taranto to ask for King Ferdinand IV of Bourbon's help.

On the 27th of may 1797, the king sent a decree ratifying freedom for the little village became free. That was the foundation day of the town of Alberobello.

History

lberobello is the heart of the trulli valley, and therefore called "Capital of the trulli". The city founded by Acquaviva Counts is a unique specimen in the world for its typical construction. Today Alberobello is a picturesque tourist and agricultural town almost made of Trulli, which give the place a great architectural relevance, together with a fairytail air of course.

The origin of the name Alberobello comes from the latin "Silva Arboris Belli" ("wood of the tree of war").

The word "Trullo" comes from the greek *tholos*, meaning "dome". Originally, the conical structure would have been built directly on the ground, but most of the surviving structure are based on perimetral walls. On the top there is a cone-shaped dome made of "chiancarelle", limestone dry laid in concentric circles and blocked by a stone named "serraglia", and by a pinnacle.

Trulli are built in dry structure, with no mortar nor any other adhesive material. The walls are about two metres high. Roof and walls are made of special limestones from the countryside.

Alberobello is counts two different districts: the so called "Rione Monti" and "Rione Aia Piccola". The first one is made up of 1000 trulli along 7 parallel roads. In this district you can see some of the most ancient Trulli, such as "trullo siamese" and the most recent Church of St. Anthony. "Rione Aia Piccola" counts about 400 peopled trulli, along some narrow streets.

The name "Aia" (farm yard) refers to a wide open space once used for threshing wheat.

The most important building is "Trullo sovrano", located in the most modern area of the city. It is made up of twelve different Trulli together. It is one of the two-storey trulli, and was built in XVIII century.

Since 1909 the "Rione Monti" has become National Monument. Later on, in 1930 also "Rione Aia Piccola" and the "Trullo Sovrano" joined the election to National Monument. In 1996 the entire city of Alberobello was declared a World Heritage Site by UNESCO.

The spread of trullo dates back to the XVIIth century, during the rule of Giangirolamo II Acquaviva d'Aragona, Count of Conversano, called by someone "the Guercio of Puglia", which aimed to develop your feud.

In 1635 he erected a dwelling for himself, still existing in Alberobello, and made a group of settlers move there, by letting them build a house, provided that this was dry-made and

not with mortar, in order to be fastly destroyed in case of royal inspection. In 1797 a group of brave citizens went to Taranto, to ask for King Ferdinando IV's help. He listened and promised. On the 27th of May of that same year the king issued a decree which set the little village free. It got redemption from feudal vassalage becoming a royal property. By then no more duty to build in trullo structure. The little village was named "Alberobello", because of an oak wood once covering that area. In Ferdinando IV square visitors can admired the first building different from a trullo: it is "Casa D'Amore", built in bricks and mortar, with a balcony in front of the Counts' house.

Alberobello offers many destinations for seightseeing: the little roads in Monti and Aia Piccola districts, along a series of *trulli* enhancing the beauty of simplicity; the Trullo Sovrano, the largest and the most important two-storied trullo; the Sanctuary of Saint Doctors Cosmas and Damien, built al the end of XIXth century; the church of St. Anthony, built in 1926 in the shape of trullo. These beautiful places welcome visitors by the fresh air and dry wind of the hills.

Events:

Folk national and international Festival "Città dei *trulli*" (First week of August);

feast of the Saint Doctors Cosmas and Damien (September 25-28);

Since decades there are some events – sort of appointments – aiming not to lose the memory of folk traditions such as historical revivals of the expulsion of Count and the "living" Christmas crib, set by the church of St. Anthony, joining the religious themes with a view of the village of the past century.

The Count of Conversano

Count Gian Girolamo II Acquaviva is considered the founder of Alberobello. He was called by someone as the "Guercio" (squinter) of Puglia. In 1635, he built a cottage for himself, and provided the country with a kiln, a mill and an inn for travellers. Close to his cottage he also built a small church dedicated to the Saint Doctors Cosmas and Damien which he was a votary of.

In order to populate the wood, he offered the farmers of the neighborhood a piece of land to cultivate and no taxes for their housings whether they built without mortar. The landowners of the neighbourhood rised up against the Count, who was violating their rights, and they asked the the king to claim his own and their rights. In 1644 the Duke of Martina Franca accused the Count of Conversano to violate the *Prammatica*. Owing to this, and expecting a visit of Royal Inspectors, in one night the Count destroyed all the "casedde", spreading the stones all around, and sending away the inhabitants.

The Trullo

History
and methods
of construction

T he name coming from the latin
words "turris" and "trulla", or from
the greek "tholos", or from greek-
byzantine "torullos", meaning "dome", the
trulli are typical buildings of millenary tradition.

Their external shape recalls the primitive
dwellings: a cone standing upon a cylinder.
All the rest of their structure stands apart.
They are completely built of stone, using no
mortar, or timber. The apparently primitive
shape hides a very ingenious plan. Trulli may
be considered the ancestral examples of the
modular constructions of the XXth century.

They can be made up of a single room, or of
different rooms, joining the first one in different stages.

The Trulli have a circular plan; along their
round perimeter there are the dry thick
walls.

The origins of the trulli

The history of these very special buildings is linked to an edict of the kingdom of Naples asking for a tribute for all new urban settlements.

The Counts of Conversano, landowners of Alberobello place, imposed the farmers to build with dry stones, with no use of mortar, in order to have precarious constructions, easy to demolish.

Having to build their housings in dry stones only, farmers found in round dome-roofed structures the easier and most convenient building solution.

The dome roofs of the trulli are embellished with decorative pinnacles, whose shape is inspired to symbolic, mystical and religious elements. They were made by the workers recruited for the construction of the trullo, and they helped identifying the craftsman. His skill and even the value of construction depended on the quality of the pinnacle. The symbols painted on the roofs often have a religious meaning; they sometimes represent zodiac signs. As regards the signs painted on the roofs, they often have a religious mean; and sometimes they may be.

Although this kind of plan reduces the available space, it makes the trullo an example of forerunning the "bio-building": the great thickness of the walls and the restricted number and small size of openings (often nothing more than a sole door and a tiny square window for the bathroom) helps keeping the air warmer during winter and fresher during summer – till the second half of August, when it begins to be warmer indoor than outdoor.

The raw material for the construction of a trullo mainly comes from the stones scattered in the countryside or from a quarry. Once he has his stones, the Trullo-builder can start to work. When necessary, a tank is excavated and completed with a barrel vault or with a dome, to receive rainwater needed for home use.

After the well, he sets the quadrangular rooms and starts building the walls – straight walls for the inside, well-squared stones for the outside. The space between the inner and the outer walls is filled with heap of stones and loam.

Once he has covered the vault, he digs the foundations, generally measuring about three meters. Then he begins to place the stones to shape the squared perimeter.

The bottom of the trullo consists of walls about two meters high; these walls are straight inside, but slightly inclined outside, like military constructions walls.

The top part is generally made with barrel vaults.

Small openings, sort of windows, are usually topped by a stone lintel, while the door requires a proper arc of dry stones carefully prepared. In the thick walls he digs room for beds and niches.

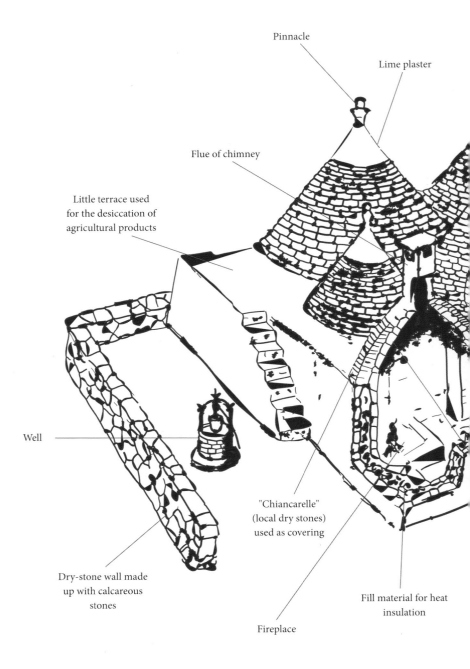

Pinnacle

Lime plaster

Flue of chimney

Little terrace used
for the desiccation of
agricultural products

Well

"Chiancarelle"
(local dry stones)
used as covering

Dry-stone wall made
up with calcareous
stones

Fireplace

Fill material for heat
insulation

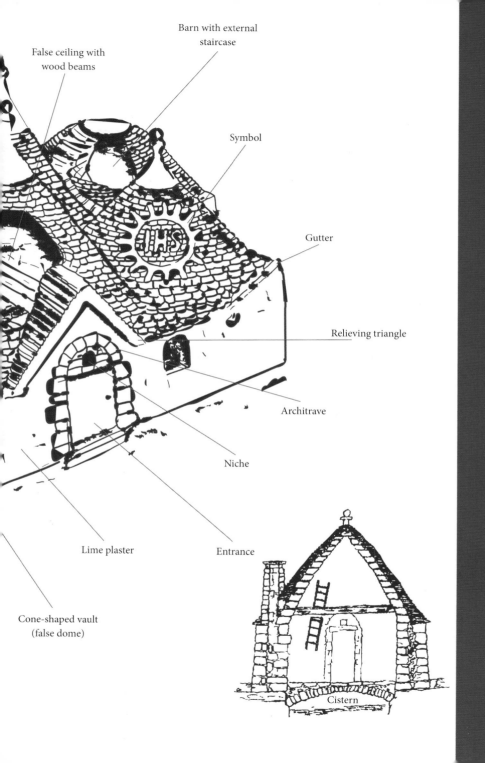

False ceiling with wood beams

Barn with external staircase

Symbol

Gutter

Relieving triangle

Architrave

Niche

Lime plaster

Entrance

Cone-shaped vault (false dome)

Cistern

To set the conic vault, which is the most important part of the trullo, at the four corners he places four large flat stones to support the weight. They are projecting and inclined to the inside of the trullo. The "Caseddaro" (trullo-builder) takes into account that four stones to stack the other flat stones, called "a candela".

Even for the construction of the vault, the "caseddaro" rarely uses any measurement systems. The stones are placed by sight.

The load-bearing walls are completed by a dome which covers the plan. This dome is a self-supporting body – meaning that it doesn't need centering. It consists of a series of concentric horizontal slabs arranged like stairs, going upward, where each complete round is statically in balance with lower ones. This inner layer of thicker slabs, called "chianche", is supplemented by an external one, which is the real roof and is made up of thinner slabs called "chiancarelle".

Generally the "chiancarelle", well-squared, were also used to pave the house.

The entrance of the trullo is characterized by two big jambs, carved in living stone, and a solid lintel, made of stone. This lintel is often topped by a niche with a religious sculpture or image.

On both sides of the door there are often two massive stone seats.

The Pinnacles

The pinnacle, cusp at the top of the cone, is a plastic and decorative element based on the circle and the triangle. Generally it is made up of three overlapping stones: the first one in cylindrical shape, the second one with a bowl or dish form, and the third one in the shape of a sphere. Its symbolic meaning is still unknown, but several hypotheses have been forwarded; somebody attributes it magic powers, someone else thinks that the pinnacle, placed on the top of the trullo, only has decorative function, according to the whims of the "trullaro"; finally, some others believe the pinnacle was a distinctive mark, imposed by the king.

Anyway, these pinnacles stand on top of all trulli, not only in Alberobello, but even on all the trulli standing in the apulian territory.

Symbols on trulli

PRIMITIVE

 Jewish seven-branched candelabrum

 Symbol containing the initial letters I and H of the name Jesus framed in a circle symbolizing the world.

 Rayed cross

 Cross cramponnée and ancient symbol for the sun

 Cross cramponnée and ancient symbol for the sun

 Symbol for the anchor, connected to the idea of salvation

Tree-cross joining the three worlds

Prayer raising to God from the earth and from hell.

Prayer raising from the earth to God

Axe-cross bringing purification and eternal life

The Star of David, a combination of two equilateral triangles

Tree cross, wishing a good and peaceful eternal life

CHRISTIAN

 The Chrismon

 Radial host with IHS inscribed – meaning Jesus

 Mary's pierced heart

 Refrigerium jar representing grace, with trefoil representing the Holy Trinity

Cross in a circle representing the universe and the sky

Symbol of sun-Christ

Cross and two pointshaving a cosmic meaning

Square inscribing an equilateral cross bearing a cosmic meaning

Lozenge inscribing an equilateral cross bearing a cosmic meaning

Cross in a circle carrying the writings "Sanctus Christus" and "Sanctus Dominus" and having the power of averting dangers

Cross set on a full square bearing a cosmic value

 Cross with obliqual segments, symbolizing divine protection

 Rayed cross bearing a cosmic meaning

 Six-armed cross surrounded by dots bearing a cosmic meaning

 Symbol considered as effective to protect against lightnings

Latin cross emphasizing the union between Gentiles and Jews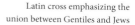

Egyptian symbol representing the female

Six armed cross with the letter iota representing Jesus

Cosmic symbol made up of three rhombs meaning God's protection over men

Cross with two horizontal branches and set on a circle bearing a cosmical meaning

 Symbol of Jupiter

 Trident representing the Holy Trinity

 Cross inscribed in an Omega representing God

 Symbol of Libra

 Symbol of Venus

 Symbol of Taurus

Symbol of Mercury

Symbol of Saturn

Trident cross, I and H representing Jesus and a circle representing the world

Symbol of Moon

Symbol of Mars

Aries constellation

The main monuments

The "Trullo Sovrano"

It is situated in the north of the country, over the monumental districts, behind the curch of Saint Doctors Cosmas and Damian. It represents the most advanced example of two-storied trullo. The big cone-shaped dome, about fourteen meters high, stands in the middle of a group of twelve cones.

Built in the first half of eighteenth century, on behalf of the wealthy family of the priest Cataldo Perta (1744-1809), therefore originally called "court of Pope Cataldo", the Trullo Sovrano is the best example of its style.

The anonymous builder, respecting the old constraints imposed by the Count Girolamo Acquaviva, built a trullo with double vault.

Unable to build both the vaults in a shape of cone without any wooden floor, he built a cross vault. The triangular pediment of the front raises to the first floor, though remaining compliant to trullo style; above the entrance door, there is an ogive arc topped with a painted moon in which a crucifix is represented.

In front of the house, in the middle of the little square, there is a tank for water.

Trullo Sovrano – outside

The skilful builder exploits every free space: he makes niches and cabinets in the walls; in the space between the ceiling of the entrance corridor and the floor of the first floor, he obtaines a large deposit of grain which becomes a safe hiding place, very useful at the time af the robbers.

Nowadays this two-storied building is a museum, and tourists can visit it, furnished in the style of past centuries, according to the oldest inhabitants' suggestions.

This prestigious building was declared national monument in 1930. It has been defined "Sovrano" not only for its majestic proportions, but also because of its extraordinary history: it was the guardian of the Blessed Sacrament and of the relics of Saints Cosmas and Damian, patrons of Alberobello.

The most important room of the house, making the difference between Trullo Sovrano and other ones, is the Living Room. A cross-vault takes the place of the usual wooden vault; this vault is completely made of stone and is supported by a system of four Romanesque arches laying on the two main walls.

The arches are used to counteract the lateral thrust of the vault and at the same time to discharge the high weight of the structure on the lateral walls. Through a bigger arch – actually closed – you could pass to other rooms originally belonging to the Trullo Sovrano. Bedroom is the smallest room. Beside the door there is a peephole (called "saitter", meaning "shooter"). It was not only used to recognize who was knocking on the door, but also to shoot the attackers.

The Rev. Father Antonio Su-

merano (1822-1895) found some chalices and other sacred objects in two niches on either sides of the window. They were walled there by the Brothers of Blessed Sacrament to save them from the frequent raids of robbers; probably, this discovery is only a little part of a great treasures that Trullo Sovrano still hides.

From the Living Room, through a corridor supporting the stairs to the top floor, you can enter the kitchen. The rectangular room seems bigger

thanks to some opening overlooking the garden, were architectural skill perfectly joins natural beauty.

On one of the short sides of the room there is an elegant fireplace, recently reconstructed during the restoration of the trullo. Previously, in its place there was a fireplace chimney that had been replaced by a less elegant and cheaper fireplace.

Inside the Trullo Sovrano you can see two twin cones communicating through an arc. But from the outside you only see the shape of a traditional trullo with a single body (obtained by filling the loop interposed between the two cones).

These rooms are the basic structure of the trullo, around which all the rest was built later. From the outside, through a secondary door, you can enter a secondary kitchen, still keeping all the main characteristics of an ancient kitchen and dining room.

Even being considered the kitchen for servants and thus less important than the other kitchen, it is a beautiful example of arch-structure. From the beginning it was an outdoor oven for baking bread, as shown by the external flues. Later on, the oven was integrated into the room, that was properly connected to the rest of trullo through a corridor.

The structure of this last room shows that the trullo Sovrano was not built as a unique body; on the contrary it comes from different stages of unification and integration that make it the best prototype of trullo architecture.

As mentioned above, the stairs help making the trullo Sovrano unique in its way: no other trullo has indoor stairs to reach the top floor.

Looking for some space to place the stairs, the unknown builder thought about this remarkable structural and architectural solution – sort of

brainwave: stairs stand in the thickness of the wall between the living room and the kitchen.

The first floor, used as a guest-room, was also used as a place for texture, frequent activity during spare time and winter for women. The trapdoor, closed by wooden lid, hides a large grain storage.

It is obtained in the space between the entrance vault of the ground floor, and the first floor ground. The rooms on the first floor have a curious recent story somehow melting with cinema and actors. Indeed, in the early 50's, being no hotels in Alberobello, the Trullo Sovrano revceived actors coming to the little town to set their movies.

Outside the trullo there is the garden, which seems to be a very attractive place for visitors, often stopping there to rest.

The garden has been furnished with tables and chairs sheltered by elegant umbrellas to enjoy a stop, among bar, restaurants and a bookshops offering the main national and international newspapers and of course books.

During the summer time, in the trullo Sovrano many cultural events take place, such as theatre performances, orchestras or jazz concerts, culture and poetry galas.

The Basilica
of Saint Doctors Cosmas and Damian

It was erected upon the original Church. The facade was built in 1885 in neoclassical style. In 1938 it became Sanctuary, and then in 2000 a minor Basilica. Thousands of devotees come to this church, above all during the period 25-28 September, to pray the Saint Doctors Cosmas and Damian.

They appeared for the first time in Alberobello, in a picture with Our Lady of Loreto. This image was preserved and venerated by Count Gian Girolamo Acquaviva, feudatory of Alberobello. In 1665 the existing church of the village became a parish church. The people from the countryside began to venerate the Saint Doctors and they celebrated them on 27 of September bringing the icon in procession. In 1782 the statue of St. Cosmas was built.

The statue coming to the town for the first time, St. Cosmas worked his first miracle: a cloudburst after a long period of drought. Two years later the statue of St. Damian was built, and both statues took the place of the old picture during the procession. From that date on, the religious ceremony has always taken place till nowadays. Over the years, the feast has become bigger, a cattle fair and a rich marketplace joined to religious ceremonies. Nowadays, after more then two centuries, the patrons' feast is still considered an important event of for people from Alberobello and closest towns.

The actual church took its actual aspect by the local Architect Antonio Curri's project (Alberobello 1848 – Napoli 1916). By a front view you can see

The facade of the Basilica

two bell towers and the 1885 façade, marked by long pilasters and fluted columns with Corinthian capitals and two smooth roman columns with composite style capitals. In 1887 the clock was installed in the left bell tower, and later, in 1906 the chapels of the Crucified, St. Joseph and the Sacred Heart were completed. The consolidation work and the inside renovation (giving the church its renaissance style) date back to 1958.

Seventeen steps get to the pronao; the image on the door, by the artist Adolfo Rollo, is drawn from the Gospel: the Beatitudes. On the left leaf, you can see the poor, the sick, the meek, those who mourn and those who hunger and thirst for justice; upon the right leaf you can see the merciful, the pure of heart, the peaceful and suffering ones.

The Portal is adorned with the four moral virtues, while the medallions represent the theological virtues; five faces of men watch at five faces of women: they are the anonymous representatives of the church. Standing up on the left side there are Matthew, Luke, Isaiah and Jeremiah; on the right side Mark and John, Ezekiel and Daniel.

In the lunette of the porch there is a bas-reliefe. It depicts Jesus Crucified with his Mother, St. John, Sts. Peter and Paul, Cosmas And Damien.

Adolfo Rollo made also the hanging crucifix on the central altar, and the big figures placed all around. Inside the church you can admire some beautiful frescoes, a chorus and an organ; the altars have been made in alabaster, a type of local marble.

The red Porphyry altar announces the Paschal Mystery of Jesus, His Death, His Resurrection (among the *Trulli*), and the Ascension; the panels standing aside represent the Annunciation and Pentecost, while in the rear triptych, the artist Giuseppe Pirrone recalls the celebration of the Vatican Council II; here you can see Pope John XXIII and Pope Paul VI.

An inscription in gold mosaic, reading "Pascha nostrum immolatus est Christus exultabunt Sancti Cosma et Damianus in gloria exeunte Concilio Vaticano II", reminds us that Jesus was sacrified for us, that the altar is dedicated to Saint Doctors, and that its erection corresponds to the completion of the Vatican Council II (1962-1965).

The frescoes in the apse are very interesting. They represents the martyrdom of the saints, and the ascent to Heaven. They were made by Francesco De Biase. The deposition, the last work by Domenico Carella, is kept in the sacristy.

The Saint Doctors Cosmas and Damian

They are generally referred to as "brothers, twins and doctors". They were able to make prodigious recoveries and miracles, and their action was completely free for everybody, so they were called "anàrgiri" (from the greek *anargyroi*, "enemy of money"). In the greek church that was the name for Saints who practiced medicine without any payment.

According to hagiographic tradition, the two twins coming from Arabia belonged to a rich family. Theyr father converted to Christianity after their birth, but was killed during a persecution, in Cilicia; their mother Theodora devoted herself to their education.

They gave their services with absolute disinterest, never asking for any wage, from both rich and poor people, following the Gospel precept: "Gratis accepistis, gratis date". One of their most famous miracles, handed down by traditions, was to replace the ulcerate leg of a sacrestan of the Basilica built on the temple of Castor and Pollux with the leg of an Ethiopian who had died short before.

They suffered a fierce martyrdom. So terrible that some martyrology talk about: "martyrs for five times". The torments suffered by Cosmas and Damian are different according to the sources. According to some sources, they were first stoned, but the stones bounced against the soldiers.

According to other sources, they were cruelly flogged, crucified, and targeted by darts, but the spears bounced without being able to hurt them.

Other sources even say they were thrown into the sea from a high cliff with a boulder attached to their neck, but the attachments were melted and the brothers could save. Some other sources report that they were put into a fiery furnace, but they weren't burned; at least they were decapitated.

44

Casa D'Amore

Wonderful building, it is the first house built with mortar, according to the project of the earlier architects of the town, in 1797. His name has nothing to do with romance. It comes from the first mayor of the city, Francesco D'Amore.

It is in trullo structure, but it is two-storied with a balcony on the top floor. It is the symbol of Alberobello redemption from feudal and despotic Acquaviva family, through the royal power. On a Stone it is written (and still visible): "Ex auctoritate regia – hoc primum erectum a.d. 1797" ("By Royal resolution, this house was the first one built with mortar").

Casa D'Amore is nowadays the seat of tourist information.

The districts

"Monti" district

It is located in the south of the town. It is made up of 1030 trulli, having about 3000 inhabitants.

Visitors can keep a wonderful view of these trulli standing on the hillside, above Largo della Foggia. Via Monte Nero and via Monte Pasubio, where the most ancient trulli take place – such as trullo Siamese – and via Monte San Michele, are the most interesting places to visit.

The "Trullo Siamese"

This trullo in double-ellipse shape, has foundations made of raw stones. Indoor there is a low-fire and no windows.

It has two different fronts, one for each trullo, overlooking two different streets.

Its story confirms its structure. Two brothers lived there together since they fell in love with the same woman. She promised her heart to the elder brother, but later on she flew away with the younger. The two brothers could not share the same trullo anymore. The elder brother drove away the two lovers, but the younger claim his legacy. So, the Trullo was divided between the two brothers. The younger brother, jealous, opened a new door for his house on the back of the trullo overlooking another street.

The Church
of St. Anthony

O n the top of Monti district, there is the church of St. Anthony, in trullo structure. It was built between 1926 and 1927 by master De Leonardis on a land donated to the priests by a woman from Alberobello. It was built under the commitment of father Anthony Lippolis (1886-1972); his idea was to put the House of God among the houses of men, therefore between Trullo houses, there is also a Trullo Church.

A deeper historical reason is linked to the spread of Protestantism in that area of the country: Christians intended to give a small center of worship to the Monti district, a poor socially disadvantaged neighbourhood.

The church was consecrated on 13 June 1927. Project and execution were all made by local craftsmen.

The dome, about 18,30 meters high, is in Trullo shape and is perfectly fitting with other buildings all around. The church has a monumental entrance preceded by a staircase and a rosette on its top; after the door visitors are immediately into the greek-cross hall; there is a bell tower, whose body has a tower structure. In the central nave there is a fresco, made by Adolfo Rollo, apulian artist, representing some Saints together with the Pantocrator Christ; there are also an important Crucifix, which stand on the altar, and the fresco behind it, representing the Tree of Life; there are also some artistic panels about the life of Saint Anthony, and a bas-reliefe about the blessed Luigi Guanella.

During 2004, the buildings has undergone substantial renovation works that restored the monuments original beauty. Nowadays the church is destination of many visitors, and many couples chose that place to celebrate their weddings. Every year, on 13 June, people in Alberobello celebrate St. Anthony, with thirteen days of prayer, called "Tredicina". These thirteen days end with the feast.

"Aia Piccola" district

It is in south-east of the town. It is composed of 400 trulli, distributed on eight streets, having more or less 1500 people living there. Very characteristic for its winding and charming streets, it has many meaningful details and corners where there is still a primitive atmosphere. The many narrow lanes are the most varied and suggestive itinerary that attracts the curiosity and attention of the tourists.

Local handicrafts

Typical activities of Alberobello are: wood, iron, clay, leather, steal, texture and pulp manufactures. in shops and souvenir-shops you can find several products Culinary art is considered a craft too. Here you can buy some of typical local production: sweet almonds, "pettole", "cartellate" and "amaretti". You should taste the typical wine and oil. People from Alberobello Inhabitants are known also for their skill in textiles art. It is still possible to purchase linen garments in the shop located between the Trulli.

The Museum of Territory

The museum rises in a very important place from a cultural and environmental point of view: The "Murgia" of Trulli and Caves. It consists of the biggest agglomerate of trulli into a unique structure (fifteen trulli), the oldest ones dating back to XVIIIth century. This residential conglomeration, called "Casa Pezzolla" from its owners name, was purchased by the municipality of Alberobello in 1986, and between 1993 and 1997 it was completely restored and brought back to its original structure. The idea of a museum was born from the desire to preserve and tell the history of the area of the Trulli, in 1996 recognized as artistic heritage of world interest by UNESCO. In "Casa Pezzolla" we can identify two different building plans: the first – most recent one – overlooking Piazza 27 Maggio, two-storied, has a high and narrow facade topped by a triangular pediment that shows the section of roof with two slopes, covered by "chiancarelle". The second one shows the most ancient part of the trullo and recalls the monuments of "Aia Piccola" district.

The museum is supposed to contain exposures of tools, findings and everything relating about the history, traditions and folklore of the area of Murgia and Trulli, but it also home to hosts exhibitions and temporary exhibitions of visual arts. The museum of territory pays a particular attention to dry stone architecture, showing methods and techniques for maintenance and restoration. There is an exposition about pinnacles, showing pinnacles of various shapes which give an idea of the peculiarities of these decorative elements. Some areas of the museum try to trace back the origins of the Trulli and the birth of Alberobello (may 27, 1797). You can see some tools used by

farmers in the early XXth century: thresher (which was used to separate the grains of wheat from the shell), forks, sickles and rakes; objects referring to the work and and urban development of the town.

Many stone handicrafts are collected. They testify the varied use of stone in Alberobello: Wheels for grinders, animal attacks, the lintel of a door, sinks, drains. There are also tools used by "Trullaro" (the trullo-builder), and the three different types of "chiancarelle". Some rooms contain an exhibition about the restoration of trulli: through a series of designs and photoss the stages of restoration of that group of trulli is shown.

Nature among the trulli

After a sightseeing of Alberobello, you can reach Bosco Selva district park, to go on a pleasant outing in a wonderful natural area.

The park is an oak wood made up of different aoks such as Fragno (*Quercus trojana*), Roverella (*Quercus pubescens*), taking place on the hillside. Through the paths that go across the field you can meet different Mediterranean botanic species, among which peony (*peonia mascula*) and wild orchids. Among the mammalians you can see the fox (*vulpes vulpes*), among the reptiles the *Elaphe quaturolineate* and the *Elaphe situla*. In the park there are also two ponds, where you can see the common frog fish (*bufo bufo*) and the newt (*Triturus italicus*). About birdlife you can see the hoopoe (*Upupa epops*) and the jay (*Garrulus glandarius*)

girovagando per
ALBEROBELLO

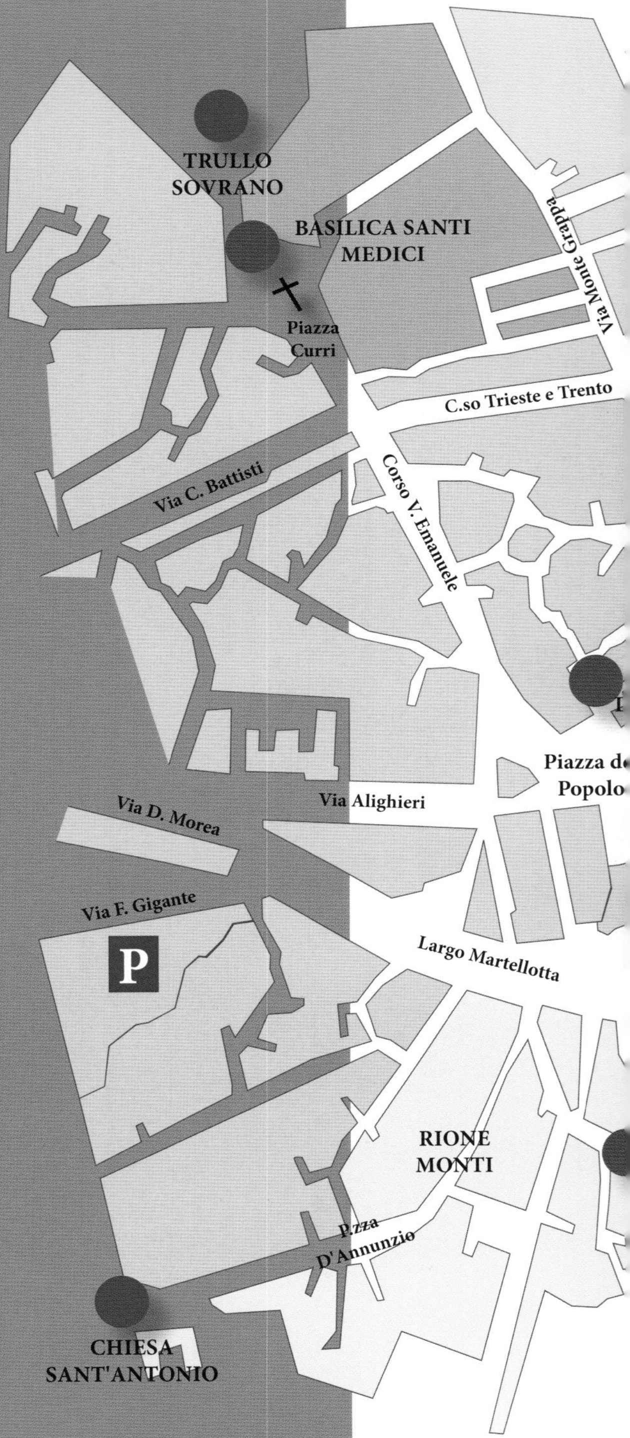

TRULLO
SOVRANO

BASILICA SANTI
MEDICI

✝

Piazza
Curri

Via Monte Grappa

C.so Trieste e Trento

Via C. Battisti

Corso V. Emanuele

Piazza del
Popolo

Via D. Morea

Via Alighieri

Via F. Gigante

P

Largo Martellotta

RIONE
MONTI

P.zza
D'Annunzio

CHIESA
SANT'ANTONIO

Le nuove guide multilingua

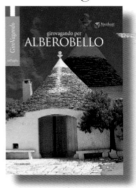

girovagando per
ALBEROBELLO

girovagando per
OSTUNI

girovagando per
BARI

Le Cartoline

ALBEROBELLO

OSTUNI

BARI

PUGLIA

I TRULLI DI PUGLIA

I BORGHI DI PUGLIA

I COLORI DI PUGLIA

LE PERLE DI PUGLIA

Le Cartine stradali

Finito di stampare nel mese di giugno 2010
dalla Sedit - Bari
per conto della GELSOROSSO